HAL LEONARD
STUDENT
PIANO
LIBRARY

MW00576497

Piano Ensembles

Four-part student ensembles with
conductor's score and optional accompaniment

LEVEL
TWO
2

Arranged by Phillip Keveren

This collection features four student favorites from
Piano Lessons Book 2 of the *Hal Leonard Student Piano Library*

TABLE OF CONTENTS

	Score	Parts				CD Tracks	GM Disk Tracks
		I	II	III	IV		
Painted Rocking Horse	3	9	11	13	15	1/2	1/2
Basketball Bounce........	5	10	12	14	16	3/4	3/4
Stompin'	17	25	27	29	31	5/6	5/6
Summer Evenings	21	26	28	30	32	7/8	7/8

Hal Leonard Student Piano Library Authors
Barbara Kreader • Fred Kern • Phillip Keveren • Mona Rejino

Piano Ensembles Level 2 is designed for use with the second book of most piano methods. Some methods
may label their second book as *Book 2* (such as the *Hal Leonard Student Piano Library*), and others may
label their second book as *Book 1*.

Concepts in *Piano Ensembles Level 2*:

Range	Symbols
	pp, p, f, mp, mf; ♯, ♭, D.S. al Fine, ⌢, ritard
Rhythm $\frac{4}{4}$ time signature	**Intervals** 2nd, 3rd, 4th and 5th melodic and harmonic

ISBN 0-7935-9215-1

HAL•LEONARD®
CORPORATION
7777 W. BLUEMOUND RD. P.O. BOX 13819 MILWAUKEE, WI 53213

Visit Hal Leonard Online at
www.halleonard.com

FOREWORD

Piano study doesn't need to be lonely any more! These ensemble versions of favorite piano pieces from the *Hal Leonard Student Piano Library* will give students the pleasure and inspiration of playing with their friends.

Each selection includes:
- A conductor's score with optional teacher accompaniment

- Four student parts:
  Parts I and II for the first piano
  Parts III and IV for the second piano

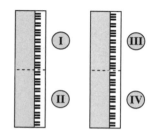

Four players at two pianos will be able to give a full and appropriate performance of each piece, yet more combinations of players and instruments are possible. Students can even add an orchestra!

Here are some ideas:
- Use four digital pianos or electronic keyboards that allow students to play the suggested instrumentation for each part.

- Double, triple, or quadruple the student parts.*

- Add the orchestral arrangement available on CD 💿 or GM disk 💾.

- Add the optional teacher accompaniment, designed for both rehearsal and performance, by using an additional piano or keyboard.

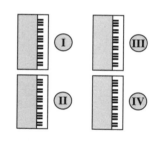

Full orchestral arrangements, available on CD #00296075 or GM disk #00296076, may be used for both performance and rehearsal:

Track 1, a **full performance version**, includes the four student parts recorded with suggested instrumentation plus an instrumental accompaniment that deepens and broadens the sound of the student ensemble.

Track 2, a **rehearsal version**, includes the four student parts recorded with suggested instrumentation and a guiding rhythm track.

If students are using a keyboard that lacks a suggested sound, other voices may be substituted. For example, if an instrument does not have "Glockenspiel," use any available similar sound, such as "Vibes" or "Marimba." If "Oboe" is unavailable, use any similar sustaining sound, such as "Flute," "Clarinet," or "Strings."

We hope you and your students will enjoy the challenges and pleasures of playing these exciting ensembles. Strike up the piano band!

Barbara Kreader   *Fred Kern*   *Phillip Keveren*   *Mona Rejino*

Due to copyright restrictions, it will be necessary to buy a new book for every four parts.

Painted Rocking Horse

Conductor's Score & Optional Accompaniment

Performance Configurations

Two Pianos   *OR*   *Four Keyboards*
(with suggested instrumentation)

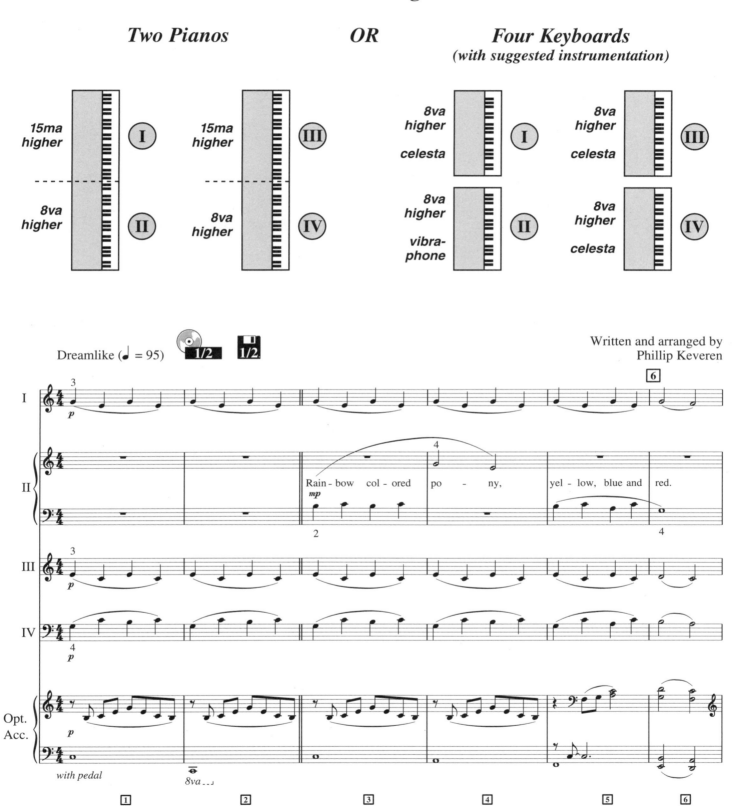

4

Basketball Bounce

Conductor's Score & Optional Accompaniment

Performance Configurations

Two Pianos

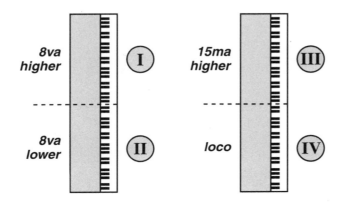

OR

Four Keyboards
(with suggested instrumentation)

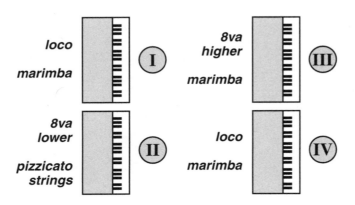

Basketball Bounce

Tempo de dribble! (♩ = 175)

Written and arranged by
Phillip Keveren

6

If you are:
- sharing the keyboard with *Part II*, **play two octaves higher**.
- seated at your own keyboard, **play one octave higher**.

Suggested instrumentation: **celesta**

Painted Rocking Horse

Part I

Dreamlike (♩ = 95)

Written and arranged by
Phillip Keveren

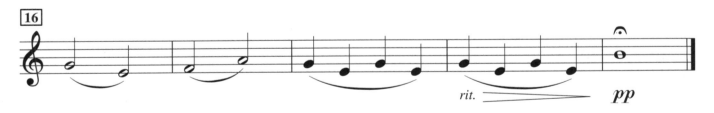

rit.   *pp*

If you are:
- sharing the keyboard with *Part II*, **play one octave higher**.
- seated at your own keyboard, **play as written**.

Suggested instrumentation:
marimba

Basketball Bounce

Part I

Written and arranged by
Phillip Keveren

Tempo de dribble! ($\quarternote$ = 175)   3/4   3/4

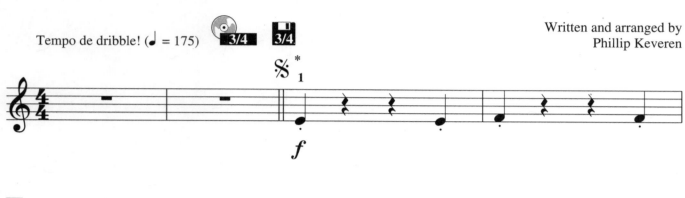

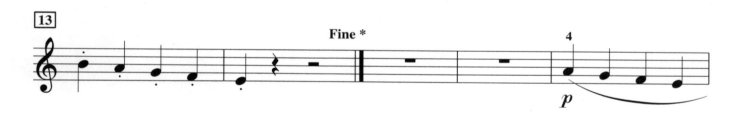

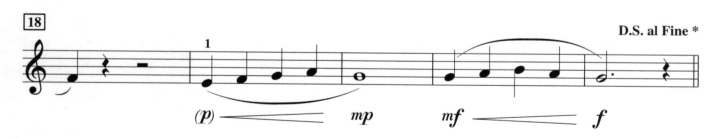

* **D.S. (Dal Segno) al Fine** means to return to 𝄋 (*segno*) and play to the end (*fine*).

DO NOT PHOTOCOPY

If you are:
- sharing the keyboard with *Part I*, **play one octave higher**.
- seated at your own keyboard, **play one octave higher**.

Suggested instrumentation:
vibraphone

Painted Rocking Horse

Part II

Dreamlike (♩ = 95)

Written and arranged by
Phillip Keveren

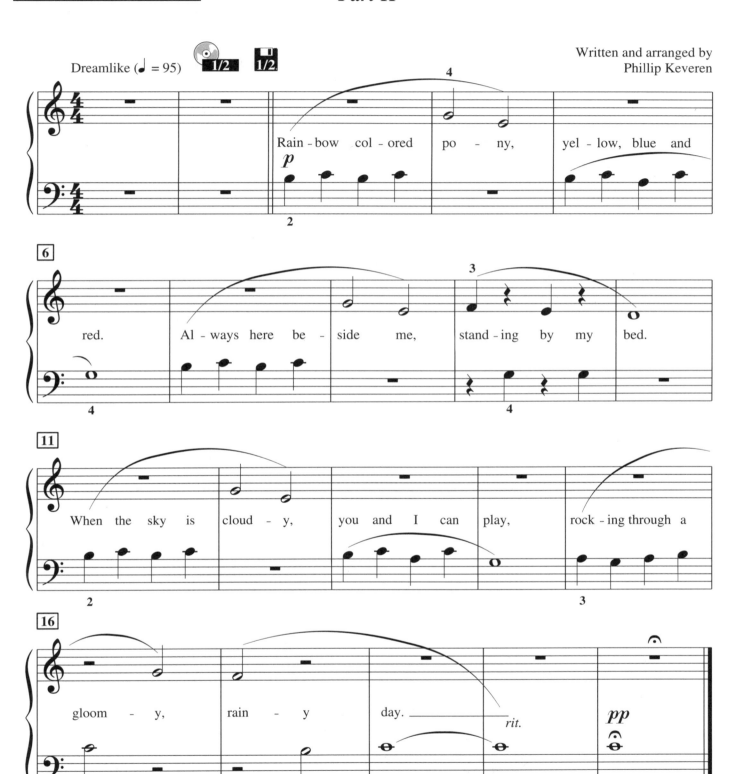

Rain - bow col - ored po - ny, yel - low, blue and red. Al - ways here be - side me, stand - ing by my bed.

When the sky is cloud - y, you and I can play, rock - ing through a gloom - y, rain - y day. *rit.* *pp*

If you are:
- sharing the keyboard with *Part I*, **play one octave lower.**
- seated at your own keyboard, **play one octave lower.**

Suggested instrumentation: **pizzicato strings**

Basketball Bounce

Part II

Written and arranged by
Phillip Keveren

Tempo de dribble! (♩ = 175)

Fine *

D.S. al Fine *

* D.S. (Dal Segno) al Fine means to return to 𝄋 (*segno*) and play to the end (*fine*).

If you are:
- sharing the keyboard with *Part IV*, **play two octaves higher**.
- seated at your own keyboard, **play one octave higher**.

Suggested instrumentation: **celesta**

Painted Rocking Horse
Part III

Written and arranged by
Phillip Keveren

Dreamlike (♩ = 95)

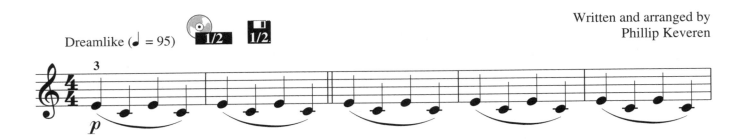

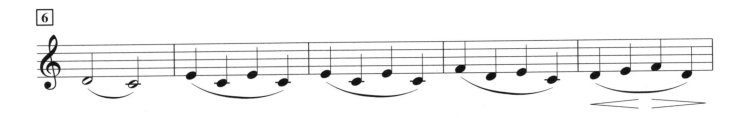

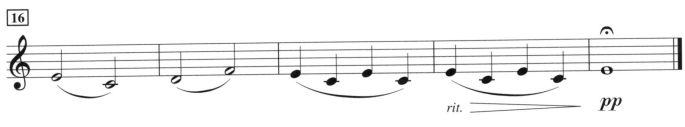

If you are:
- sharing the keyboard with *Part IV*, **play two octaves higher**.
- seated at your own keyboard, **play one octave higher**.

Suggested instrumentation:
marimba

Basketball Bounce

Part III

Written and arranged by
Phillip Keveren

Tempo de dribble! (♩ = 175) 3/4 3/4

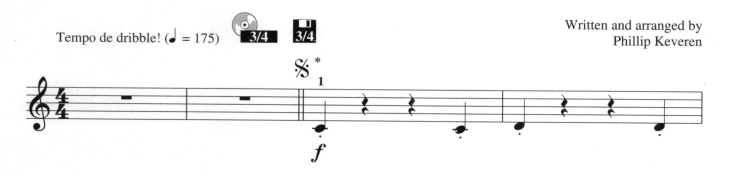

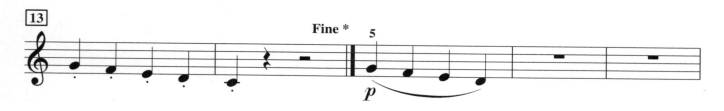

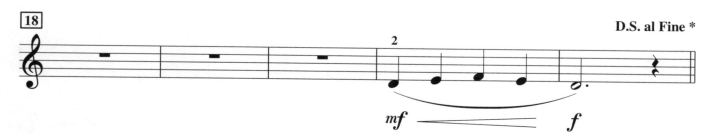

* **D.S. (Dal Segno) al Fine** means to return to 𝄋 (*segno*) and play to the end (*fine*).

DO NOT PHOTOCOPY

14

If you are:
- sharing the keyboard with *Part III*, **play one octave higher**.
- seated at your own keyboard, **play one octave higher**.

Suggested instrumentation:
celesta

Painted Rocking Horse

Part IV

Written and arranged by
Phillip Keveren

Dreamlike (♩ = 95)

rit. *pp*

If you are:
- sharing the keyboard with *Part III*,
  play as written.
- seated at your own keyboard,
  play as written.

Suggested instrumentation:
marimba

Basketball Bounce

Part IV

Written and arranged by
Phillip Keveren

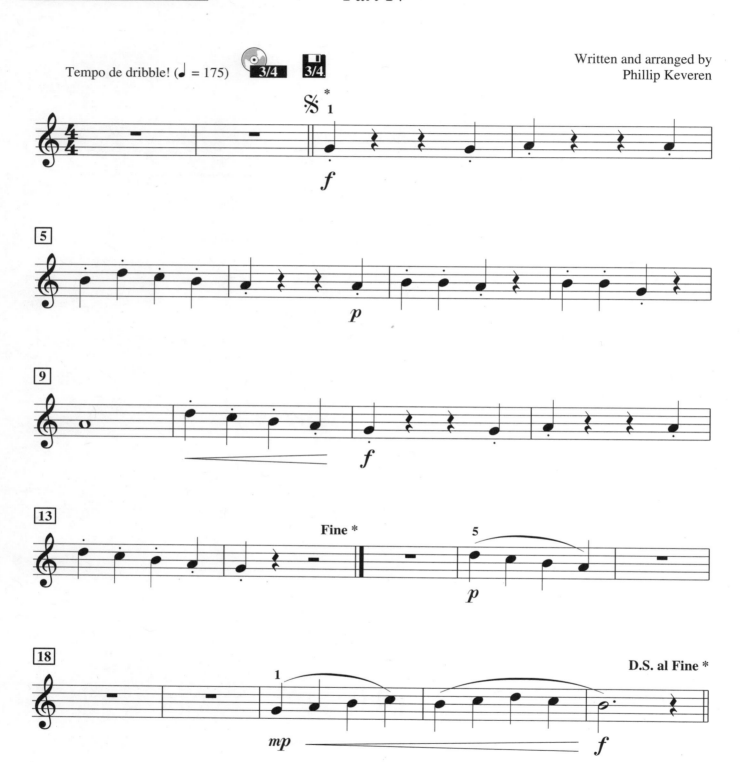

Tempo de dribble! (♩ = 175)

* **D.S. (Dal Segno) al Fine** means to return to 𝄋 (*segno*) and play to the end (*fine*).

DO NOT PHOTOCOPY

Stompin'

Conductor's Score & Optional Accompaniment

Performance Configurations

Two Pianos

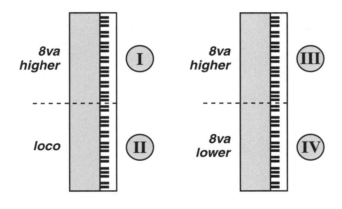

8va higher   I

loco   II

8va higher   III

8va lower   IV

OR

Four Keyboards
(with suggested instrumentation)

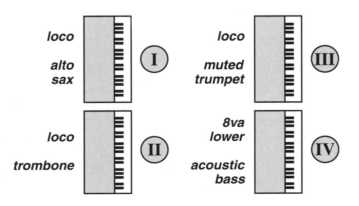

loco
alto sax   I

loco
trombone   II

loco
muted trumpet   III

8va lower
acoustic bass   IV

Stompin'

Bill Boyd
Arranged by Phillip Keveren

Summer Evenings

Conductor's Score & Optional Accompaniment

Performance Configurations

Two Pianos

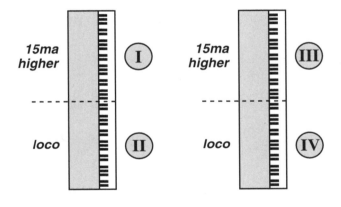

15ma higher   ①

loco   ②

15ma higher   ③

loco   ④

OR

Four Keyboards
(with suggested instrumentation)

8va higher

celesta   ①

8va higher

music box   ③

loco

harp   ②

8va higher

music box   ④

Summer Evenings

"Alouette"
Arranged by Phillip Keveren

If you are:
- sharing the keyboard with *Part II*, **play one octave higher**.
- seated at your own keyboard, **play as written**.

Suggested instrumentation:
alto sax

Stompin'

Part I

Bill Boyd
Arranged by Phillip Keveren

Keep the beat! (♩ = 190)

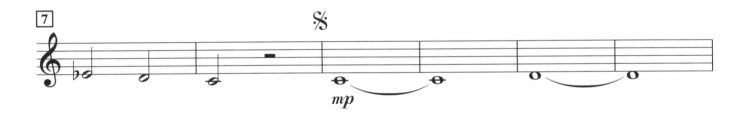

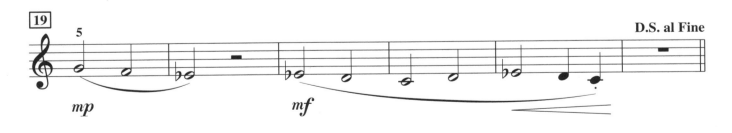

If you are:
- sharing the keyboard with *Part II*, **play two octaves higher**.
- seated at your own keyboard, **play one octave higher**.

Suggested instrumentation: **celesta**

Summer Evenings

Part I

"Alouette"
Arranged by Phillip Keveren

Sweetly (♩ = 130)

Play on repeat only

If you are:
- sharing the keyboard with *Part I*, **play as written**.
- seated at your own keyboard, **play as written**.

Suggested instrumentation: **trombone**

Stompin'

Part II

Bill Boyd
Arranged by Phillip Keveren

Keep the beat! (♩ = 190)   5/6   5/6

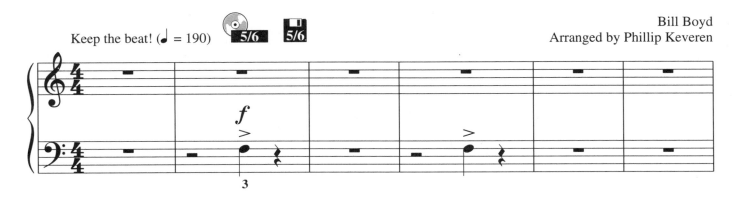

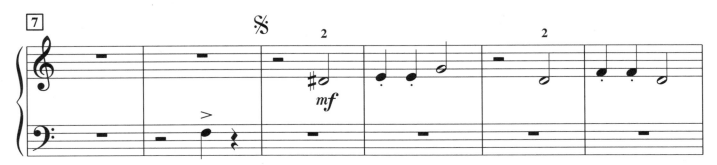

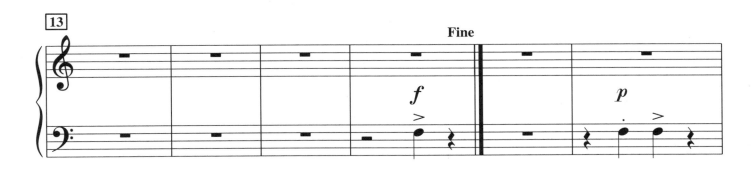

If you are:
- sharing the keyboard with *Part I*, **play as written**.
- seated at your own keyboard, **play as written**.

Suggested instrumentation: **harp**

Summer Evenings

Part II

"Alouette"
Arranged by Phillip Keveren

Sweetly (♩ = 130)

If you are:
- sharing the keyboard with *Part IV*, **play one octave higher**.
- seated at your own keyboard, **play as written**.

Suggested instrumentation: **muted trumpet**

Stompin'
Part III

Bill Boyd
Arranged by Phillip Keveren

Keep the beat! (♩ = 190)   5/6   5/6

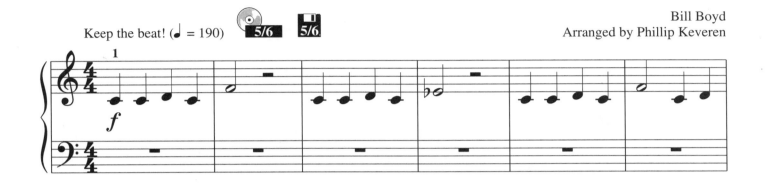

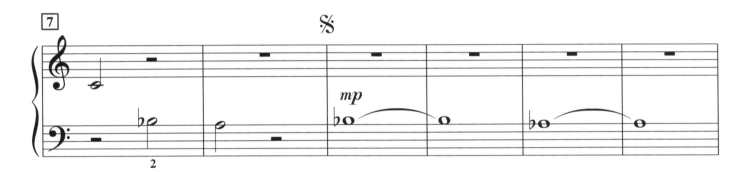

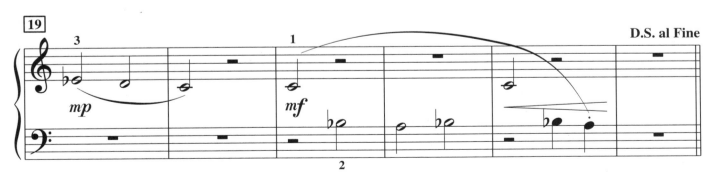

© Hal Leonard

29

If you are:
- sharing the keyboard with *Part IV*, **play two octaves higher**.
- seated at your own keyboard, **play one octave higher**.

Suggested instrumentation: **music box**

Summer Evenings
Part III

"Alouette"
Arranged by Phillip Keveren

Sweetly (♩ = 130)   7/8   7/8

(Count 8 measures of rest.)

If you are:
- sharing the keyboard with *Part III*, **play one octave lower**.
- seated at your own keyboard, **play one octave lower**.

Suggested instrumentation: **acoustic bass**

Stompin'
Part IV

Bill Boyd
Arranged by Phillip Keveren

Keep the beat! (♩ = 190)

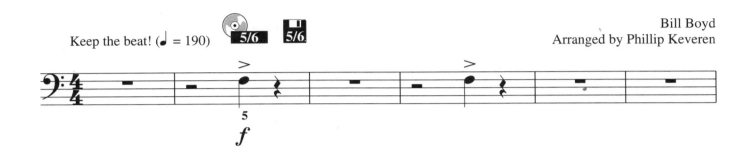

Fine

D.S. al Fine

© Hal Leonard

If you are:
- sharing the keyboard with *Part III*, **play as written.**
- seated at your own keyboard, **play one octave higher.**

Suggested instrumentation: **music box**

Summer Evenings
Part IV

"Alouette"
Arranged by Phillip Keveren

Sweetly (♩ = 130)

(Count 8 measures of rest.)

Sum - mer eve - nings, moon - light through my win - dow. Star - light

shin - ing, breez - es blow - ing sighs. As I lie up - on my bed,

sights and sounds soon fill my head. Light - ning bugs, pass - ing cars, crick - et calls,

fall - ing stars. Sum - mer eve - nings warm and soft and still.